EXTREME SPORTS
SNOWBOARDING

by Tracy Vonder Brink

pogo

Ideas for Parents and Teachers

Pogo Books let children practice reading informational text while introducing them to nonfiction features such as headings, labels, sidebars, maps, and diagrams, as well as a table of contents, glossary, and index.

Carefully leveled text with a strong photo match offers early fluent readers the support they need to succeed.

Before Reading

- "Walk" through the book and point out the various nonfiction features. Ask the student what purpose each feature serves.
- Look at the glossary together. Read and discuss the words.

Read the Book

- Have the child read the book independently.
- Invite them to list questions that arise from reading.

After Reading

- Discuss the child's questions. Talk about how they might find answers to those questions.
- Prompt the child to think more. Ask: Would you like to try snowboarding? Why or why not?

Pogo Books are published by Jump!
5357 Penn Avenue South
Minneapolis, MN 55419
www.jumplibrary.com

Copyright © 2025 Jump!
International copyright reserved in all countries. No part of this book may be reproduced in any form without written permission from the publisher.

Library of Congress Cataloging-in-Publication Data

Names: Vonder Brink, Tracy, author.
Title: Snowboarding / by Tracy Vonder Brink.
Description: Minneapolis, MN: Jump!, Inc., [2025]
Series: Extreme sports | Includes index.
Audience: Ages 7–10
Identifiers: LCCN 2024035259 (print)
LCCN 2024035260 (ebook)
ISBN 9798892136457 (hardcover)
ISBN 9798892136464 (paperback)
ISBN 9798892136471 (ebook)
Subjects: LCSH: Snowboarding–Juvenile literature.
Physics–Juvenile literature.
Classification: LCC GV857.S57 V66 2025 (print)
LCC GV857.S57 (ebook)
DDC 796.939–dc23/eng/20240816
LC record available at https://lccn.loc.gov/2024035259
LC ebook record available at https://lccn.loc.gov/2024035260

Editor: Alyssa Sorenson
Designer: Molly Ballanger

Photo Credits: Artranq/iStock, cover; muroPhotographer/Shutterstock, 1; MyImages - Micha/Shutterstock, 3; AscentXmedia/iStock, 4; lzf/Shutterstock, 5; Benoist/Shutterstock, 6-7; Eric Bergeri/iStock, 8-9; Mariusz Pietranek/Dreamstime, 10; Iankovskii Ian/Dreamstime, 11; hurricanehank/Shutterstock, 12-13; Dmytro Vietrov/Shutterstock, 14-15; Francesco Vaninetti/Dreamstime, 16; MARCO BERTORELLO/AFP/Getty, 17; Cavan Images/Alamy, 18-19; Cameron Spencer/Getty, 20-21; bullet74/Shutterstock, 23.

Printed in the United States of America at Corporate Graphics in North Mankato, Minnesota.

TABLE OF CONTENTS

CHAPTER 1
Speeding Down Slopes................4

CHAPTER 2
Slopestyle Skills................10

CHAPTER 3
Half-Pipe Tricks................16

ACTIVITIES & TOOLS
Try This!................22
Glossary................23
Index................24
To Learn More................24

CHAPTER 1
SPEEDING DOWN SLOPES

A snowboarder rides up a snow-covered ramp. They twist and flip in the air. How? They use **physics** to do **gravity**-defying tricks!

ramp

Snowboarders ride down snowy mountains or other **slopes** on snowboards. They often bend their knees. Why? This lowers their **center of gravity**. It helps them balance.

A snowboard has metal edges. When the board turns, the metal digs into the snow. This increases **traction**. It helps the snowboarder control the board.

TAKE A LOOK!

What are the parts of a snowboard? Take a look!

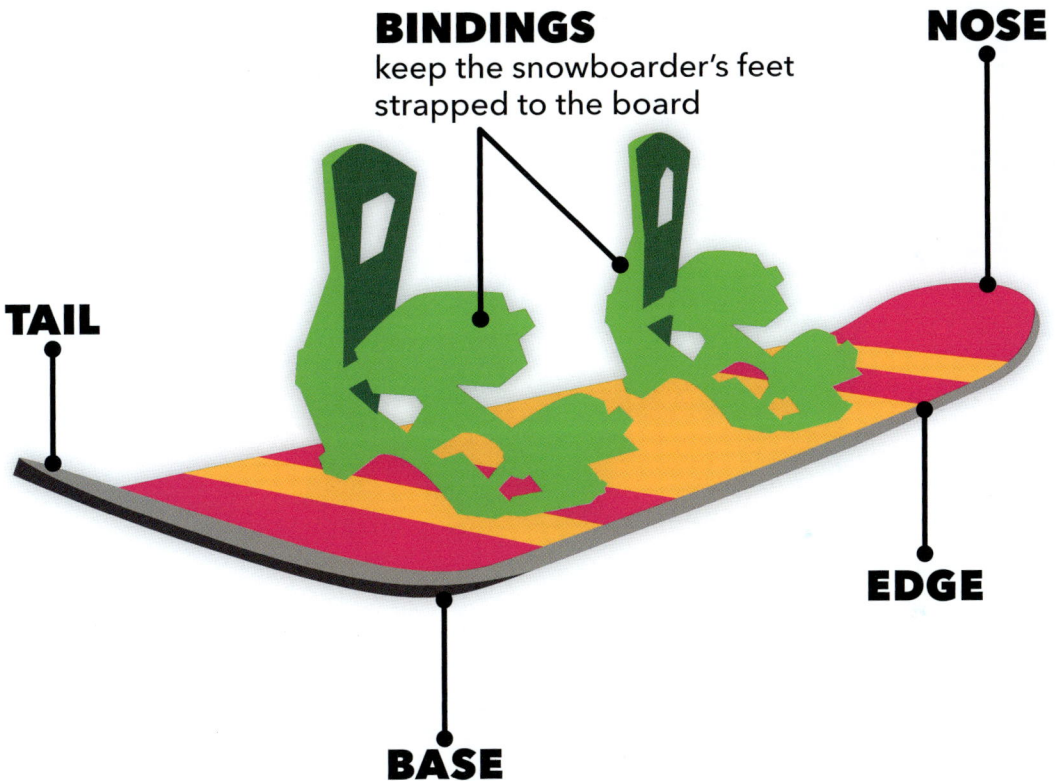

BINDINGS keep the snowboarder's feet strapped to the board

NOSE

TAIL

EDGE

BASE

A snowboarder starts at the top of a slope. Gravity pulls them to the bottom. The board rubs on snow as it slides. This creates **friction** and heat. It melts the snow a bit. The snowboarder **glides** on a thin layer of water. They go fast!

DID YOU KNOW?

Snowboarders can go 60 miles (97 kilometers) per hour!

CHAPTER 2
SLOPESTYLE SKILLS

Slopestyle is a type of snowboarding. There is a course on the slope. It has ramps and rails. Snowboarders do tricks on their way down.

Some butter. To do this, a snowboarder leans back. Moving their weight lifts the board's nose off the ground. The board glides smoothly on top of the snow!

Jibbing is another trick. A snowboarder comes to a rail. They lift their feet and the board. They jump onto the rail. **Momentum** keeps the board moving forward. It slides!

DID YOU KNOW?

Snowboarders bend their knees when they land tricks. Why? This helps **absorb** the **impact**. It keeps their legs from getting hurt.

Some snowboarders do a trick called the wildcat. They go up a ramp. They lean back. At the top, they twist their shoulders. Why? This starts their spin. In the air, the snowboarder tucks their body. They grab the board with one hand. They **rotate** into a backflip!

DID YOU KNOW?

The wildcat and other tricks take practice. Some snowboarders practice backflips on a trampoline first!

CHAPTER 2

CHAPTER 3
HALF-PIPE TRICKS

A half-pipe curves on both ends. The boarder drops in. Sliding down one side gives them momentum to zoom up the other side.

half-pipe

They **pump**. Why? This helps them go even faster. To pump, a snowboarder bends their knees at the bottom of the half-pipe. They straighten as they go up the other side. Changing their center of gravity builds speed. Speed helps them do tricks.

CHAPTER 3

A handplant is a half-pipe trick. The boarder goes up the half-pipe. They reach the edge. Their board goes into the air. The snowboarder puts their hand down. This stops their momentum. They go upside down!

TAKE A LOOK!

What are the steps of a handplant? Take a look!

① **A snowboarder goes up the half-pipe.**

② **The board goes over the edge of the half-pipe and into the air.**

③ **The snowboarder puts their hand down. Their upper body stops moving. Their feet and board go into the air.**

④ **The snowboarder is upside down! The board is above them.**

⑤ **They bring the board back down. They let go of the edge.**

⑥ **They zoom back down the half-pipe.**

Snowboarding takes practice. Some people practice for years. The most talented go to the Olympics. They **compete**. The best snowboarder gets a gold medal. Physics helps them win!

ACTIVITIES & TOOLS

TRY THIS!

FRICTION TEST

Friction melts snow under a moving snowboard. Explore how it works with this fun activity!

What You Need:
- 1 ice cube
- a dry countertop
- 3 sticky notes

1. Put the ice cube on the counter with a flat side down.
2. Push the ice cube. Mark where it stops with a sticky note.
3. Rub the ice cube back and forth until the bottom starts to melt. It should be wet but not dripping.
4. Push the ice cube again. Mark where it stops with a sticky note.
5. Rub the ice cube back and forth until the bottom melts enough to drip.
6. Push the ice cube again. Mark where it stops with a sticky note.
7. Compare where your three notes are. When did the ice cube move the farthest? Why do you think that is?

GLOSSARY

absorb: To take in.

center of gravity: The point on an object at which half of its weight is on one side and half is on the other.

compete: To try to win a contest.

friction: The force that slows down objects when they rub against each other.

glides: Moves smoothly.

gravity: The force that pulls things toward the center of Earth and keeps them from floating away.

impact: The action of one object hitting another with force.

momentum: The force or speed something gains as it moves.

physics: The science that deals with matter, energy, and their interactions.

pump: A snowboarding technique in which a change in body position helps the snowboarder gain speed.

rotate: To turn around a center point.

slopes: Pieces of land that slant downward.

traction: The force that keeps a moving body from slipping on a surface.

ACTIVITIES & TOOLS   23

INDEX

balance 5
butter 11
center of gravity 5, 17
control 6
friction 8
glides 8, 11
gravity 4, 8
half-pipe 16, 17, 18, 19
handplant 18, 19
impact 13
jibbing 13
momentum 13, 16, 18

mountains 5
Olympics 21
physics 4, 21
practice 14, 21
pump 17
rails 10, 13
ramp 4, 10, 14
slopes 5, 8, 10
slopestyle 10
traction 6
tricks 4, 10, 13, 14, 17, 18
wildcat 14

TO LEARN MORE

Finding more information is as easy as 1, 2, 3.
❶ Go to www.factsurfer.com
❷ Enter "snowboarding" into the search box.
❸ Choose your book to see a list of websites.